DK **eyewonder**

Whales
and Dolphins

LONDON, NEW YORK, MUNICH,
MELBOURNE, and DELHI

Written and edited by Caroline Stamps
Designed by Helen Chapman and Cheryl Telfer
Publishing manager Susan Leonard
Managing art editor Clare Sheddon
US editor Margaret Parrish
Picture researcher Bridget Tily
Production Shivani Pandey
DTP designer Almudena Díaz
Consultant Kim Dennis-Bryan PhD, FZS
With thanks to Venice Shone for artwork.

REVISED EDITION
DK UK
Senior editor Caroline Stamps
Senior art editor Rachael Grady
Jacket design Natasha Rees
Producer (print production) Rita Sinha
Producers (pre-production)
Francesca Wardell, Rachel Ng
Publisher Andrew Macintyre

DK INDIA
Senior editor Priyanka Nath
Senior art editor Rajnish Kashyap
Art editor Isha Nagar
Assistant editor Deeksha Saikia
Managing editor Alka Thakur Hazarika
Managing art editor Romi Chakraborty
DTP designer Anita Yadav
Picture researcher Sumedha Chopra

First American Edition, 2003
This American Edition, 2013
Published in the United States by
DK Publishing
375 Hudson Street
New York, New York 10014
13 14 15 16 17 10 9 8 7 6 5 4 3 2 1
001—192749—05/2013

A catalog record for this book is available
from the Library of Congress.
ISBN 978-1-4654-0910-2

DK books are available at special discounts when purchased in bulk
for sales promotions, premiums, fund-raising, or educational use. For
details, contact: DK Publishing Special Markets, 375 Hudson Street,
New York, New York 10014 or SpecialSales@dk.com.

Color reproduction by Scanhouse, Malaysia
Printed and bound in China by Hung Hing

Discover more at
www.dk.com

Contents

A mammal, not a fish

All of the animals on these pages are able to glide through the water, but they are not fish. They are warm-blooded mammals, just like us. They have lungs, not gills, and must come to the surface to breathe air.

Breathe in
Whales and dolphins draw air into their lungs through a blowhole, not through their mouths. The blowhole is positioned on top of their heads.

We like milk!

Baby sea lions, like all mammals, suckle their mother's milk. The nipples are hidden in slits on the mother's belly. The rich milk is about 50 percent fat.

Whale's milk is about 10 times richer in fat than cow's milk.

Blubber for warmth

Many whales, dolphins, and seals live in icy places. Under the skin, a thick, oily fat called blubber protects them from the cold.

Sea lion's milk is as thick as mayonnaise. A pup will suckle for up to a year.

A baby seal's white fur helps to hide it.

Helping hair

Seals and sea lions have sensitive whiskers that help them to find their food because they pick up on movement under the water.

As it dives, a seal expels all the air from its lungs.

Taking a breath

Because they are mammals, whales, dolphins, and seals all have to come to the surface to breathe. How long they stay underwater after taking a breath varies from a few minutes to about two hours, depending on the species.

Some seal species can dive to depths of more than 3,000 ft (900 m).

Strong muscles around the blowhole close it before the animal dives.

One hole...

A whale's blowhole—a muscular opening that leads to the animal's lungs—is positioned on the top of its head. Toothed whales, such as orcas, belugas, and dolphins, have only one blowhole.

... or two

Baleen whales, such as the humpback, have two blowholes. The skin around the blowhole is very sensitive, so the whale knows when it is clear of the water and it is safe to open it.

Going down empty

A seal is unusual because it breathes out as it dives, closing its nostrils and blocking its windpipe so that it dives with empty lungs. Oxygen from the air has already entered its blood supply and is feeding its brain and muscles.

A seal might stay underwater for about 70 minutes.

"Thar, she blows!"

When a whale surfaces, it breathes out rapidly producing a "blow" or "spout," which is a spray of seawater. A large whale's blow can be up to 13 ft (4 m) high and can be seen several miles away.

Air facts

- A humpback can hold its breath for 30 minutes, but will usually surface every 4–10 minutes.

- Sperm whales stay underwater for up to 75 minutes.

In the 1800s, whalers could recognize the type of whale by the height and direction of its blow.

Swift swimmers

Whales are the sprinters of the oceans, using their tails to power forward. Unlike land mammals, different whales share the same basic shape. It's the best shape for cruising through the water.

The dorsal fin helps to stop a whale from rolling in the water.

Dolphins live in schools of up to 1,000 animals. They twist and turn continually to avoid collisions.

Let's play

Dolphins have lots of fun riding the bow waves of boats and ships, or swimming in the frothy wake, jostling for position.

Built for speed

Orcas are the fastest of all sea mammals, but most whales are pretty swift swimmers. Their torpedo-shaped bodies are perfect for cutting through the water.

A short, stiff neck helps the whale to swim fast.

Different species of whale have differently shaped beaks. Some have no beak at all.

A stiff neck

Some whales, such as the orca, cannot turn their heads from side to side because their neck bones are fused together. This is a useful adaptation to life in the water and allows the whale to reach high speeds.

A whale's front flippers, or forelimbs, are used to change direction.

A streamlined body helps the whale to swim.

Left a bit, right a bit...

The large front flippers help to control direction. A dolphin shows how effective this is when picking off small fish from a large school.

Up, down, up, down

A whale's tail moves up and down to push the animal through the water, unlike a fish, whose tail moves from side to side.

Powerful muscles tighten and relax to pull the tail up and down.

A great tail

A whale's tail is made up of two tail flukes, or sections, that are joined at the center. Unlike a fish's tail, a whale's tail lies flat. This is the whale's "propeller," which forces it forward.

What a leap!
The sheer power of the tail's muscle is shown by the fact that many whales and dolphins can launch themselves out of the water.

Listen up!
A whale will sometimes slap its tail flukes against the water's surface. It is thought that this may be a form of communication.

A whale's skin feels as smooth and rubbery as a hard-boiled egg.

Flying through the water
A whale's tail flukes are thicker at the front than at the back, just like an aircraft's wing. It helps the flukes to slide through the water.

It's all in the tail

Humpback whales have special markings under their flukes. Since every humpback is different, scientists can recognize individual whales.

A whale's tail is full of tiny blood vessels that help to cool the animal down.

Muscle power

Most of the back third of a whale's body is made up of muscle. The muscle is connected to the backbone.

Dancing dolphins

Dolphins form spectacular displays as they leap out of the water. They are often friendly to humans and can be incredibly nosy. There are about 26 different types, or species. One way of identifying different species is through their markings.

Dolphins take a breath as they leap out of the water, but continue to swim forward. This leap-swim action is called "porpoising."

Bottlenose dolphins can leap several yards into the air.

A friend to all
Bottlenose dolphins are one of the best-known of all dolphins, and there are many stories of them helping people in trouble.

A porpoise, not a dolphin

There are six different types of porpoise—this is the harbor porpoise. Porpoises are very shy and, unlike dolphins, tend to swim alone. Their heads are blunt, with no beak.

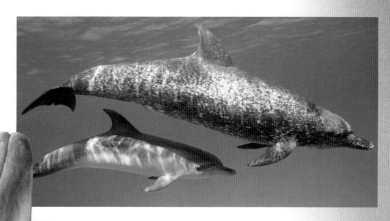

Spot those spots

Spotted dolphins are born without spots, but develop them as they grow. They appear first on the newborn dolphin's belly and spread up.

The longest beak

River dolphins have surprisingly long beaks and, unlike many whales, can turn their heads. Both these features help them to poke around on the riverbed for food.

A river dolphin has tiny eyes and finds its way using echolocation.

Scarred for life

It's easy to identify a Risso's dolphin—it is covered in white scars. The scars are caused by fights with other Risso's dolphins.

Risso's is one of the few dolphins with a blunt head.

13

Teeth

Whales can be split into those that have teeth (toothed whales) and those that don't (baleen whales). Toothed whales, such as the sperm whale or the dolphin, have simple, peglike teeth that are all the same shape.

A sperm whale's tooth can weigh over 2 lb (1 kg). That's more than double the weight of this book!

Teeth for life

A dolphin's teeth grow in a single row on the upper and lower jaw. It has the same set for life, so if a tooth is lost, it will not be replaced.

Whose teeth?

These teeth belonged to a full-grown sperm whale. Sperm whales have the largest teeth of all the toothed whales. They grow up to 8 in (20 cm) in length.

A sperm whale has teeth only in its lower jaw.

The crabeater seal's teeth close to form a sieve that filters food from the water.

All the better to eat you

A seal doesn't chew. It uses its teeth to grasp and bite, and it swallows its prey whole. Seals hunt and eat in water.

Not all the same

Seals and sea lions have a range of different teeth, just like us. This crabeater seal shows its incisors, canines, and jagged cheek teeth (which are adapted premolars and molars).

Canine tooth

How old?

It is possible to tell the age of some whales and seals by looking at cross-sections of their teeth. Just like a tree, one ring means one year of growth.

15

The filter feeders

Some of the largest whales have no teeth. Instead, they filter their food from the sea through fringed brushes called baleen plates that hang down inside their mouths.

Big appetite, small food
Despite their size, the whales that filter food eat enormous quantities of tiny, shrimplike creatures called krill. Each is no longer than your finger.

A humpback whale's baleen is about 40 in (100 cm) in length.

In the groove
Some filter feeders, such as these humpbacks, have throat grooves. These allow their mouths and throats to expand to take in tons of water.

The whales take huge gulps of seawater and food, then strain out the food.

Humpback whales fish in groups of up to 25.

A big brush

Baleen plates grow in rows from the upper jaw. The stiff hairs act as a filter.

Bubble nets

One way that humpbacks catch their food is by releasing air to make bubble nets. These air cages trap fish and plankton.

A humpback may have 800 baleen plates.

Each humpback has between 10 and 36 throat grooves below its mouth.

Filter facts

● Before birth, baleen whales have tiny tooth buds, but these never develop into teeth.

● Baleen is made of keratin, the same material as human fingernails!

● Just like your fingernails, baleen is constantly growing.

Family life

Adult whales and dolphins make protective parents when it comes to the safety of their young. Many travel around in close-knit families called pods and prefer to do their feeding in social groups.

Sperm whale mothers and calves form large nursery "schools."

Babysitting services

Female sperm whales live together in big groups with their young calves. When the mother dives to seek food, another female will babysit the calf and protect it from sharks or killer whales.

Join the club

The relationships built between orcas from the same pod last for life. They hunt together, sharing the winnings, and care for each other's young, sick, or injured.

A warm start

A female humpback nurses its newborn calf in warm, shallow waters. The calf feeds on its mother's rich, fatty milk.

Sperm whale calves usually suckle their mother's milk for just over two years.

Sperm whales can live for 70 years.

Whale facts

● Humpback whale calves may grow as quickly as 1½ ft (0.5 m) every month.

● If a baby dolphin strays too far from the mother, she may "punish" it by trapping the infant between her flippers for a few seconds.

Sperm whale calves are born tail first.

Always close to home

A newborn dolphin is nursed by its mother for as long as a year and a half. During this time, the baby hardly ever leaves its mother's side.

19

Humpbacks have the longest flippers of any whale.

Communication

Listen to a pod of whales, and you will hear a lot of clicking and whistling. It's their way of "talking." There are other ways that whales and dolphins "talk."

I'm here!

Slapping a flipper against the water's surface is one way of getting attention, especially when the flipper belongs to a humpback whale.

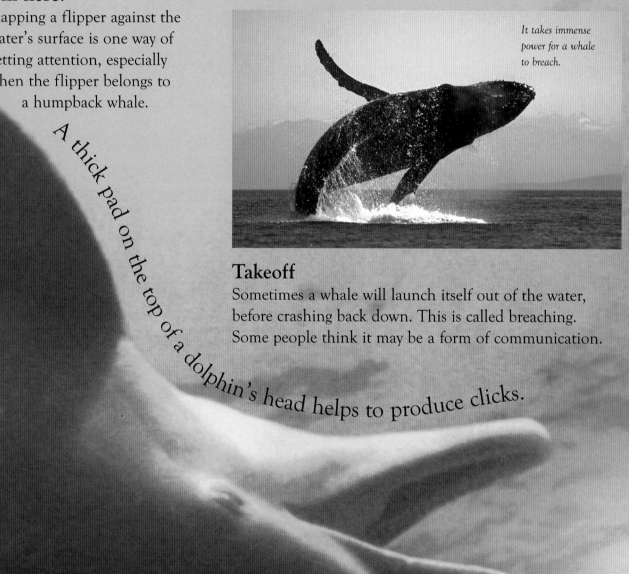

It takes immense power for a whale to breach.

Takeoff

Sometimes a whale will launch itself out of the water, before crashing back down. This is called breaching. Some people think it may be a form of communication.

A thick pad on the top of a dolphin's head helps to produce clicks.

Bubble soup

The bubbles are a sign that this male humpback whale has found a female. The males also sing. Scientists believe that the sound helps them to find a mate.

A big argument

It's not unusual to see a pair of dolphins "chattering" away to each other, mouths open. A confrontation like this usually means an argument.

These clicks help a dolphin to find things. It's called echolocation.

I see you

Some whales will rise up slowly to peep above the water's surface. This is called spy hopping. It shows just how curious many whales are about the world above the water.

A WHALE IN SPACE

A recording of humpback whale songs was put aboard the *Voyager* space probe in 1977 as a greeting from Earth. The songs are the most complex in the animal kingdom.

On the move

Many whales move, or migrate, to find food or to find a mate. Some make amazing journeys, traveling thousands of miles. This map shows some of the journeys that they make.

Which way?

Whales use ocean currents, Earth's magnetic field, the seabed, and the position of the Sun to help them find their way.

ARCTIC

Gray whales

One of the longest journeys of any mammal is made by the gray whale—this whale makes a round trip of more than 12,000 miles (20,000 km).

Many sperm whale migrations happen because they are following their favorite food, squid. Where the squid go, the whales follow.

ANTARCTIC

Sperm whales

Male sperm whales spend most of the year in icy polar seas. They head to the tropics to find females, who tend to stay in warmer waters.

Narwhals

Narwhals live in Arctic seas. Their movements follow shifts and breakups in the Arctic pack ice, which depend on the season.

When narwhals are on the move, they swim close to the surface.

Hot or cold?

The pink band shows the warmest parts of the Earth—the area around the equator. The Arctic and Antarctic—the poles—are the coldest.

Humpback whales

Like the gray whale, humpbacks migrate huge distances. They feed in polar seas (the map shows two Antarctic populations) and move to warmer seas to mate and give birth.

When migrating, many whales may go without food for three, four, or even five months.

23

A baleen whale's jawbone is far larger than that of a toothed whale.

What a whopper!

The blue whale's massive jawbones are sometimes erected as arches. Here they frame a doorway of a popular fisheries museum in Nova Scotia, Canada.

A peek inside

Whale bones are more porous than our bones and contain a lot of oil. Oil floats in water, so the huge quantities inside a whale help its buoyancy, or ability to float, in water.

Hidden protection

Just like a human skeleton, a whale's skeleton has a backbone and a long, slender rib cage that protects the delicate internal organs.

Orca skeleton

Is it a dog?

A seal's skeleton is more like a dog's than a whale's. It even has hind limb bones in its tail flipper.

Elephant seal skeleton

A whale has a shoulder blade, or scapula.

Human shoulder blade

A ball-and-socket joint allows all-around movement.

Strong flippers

The bones in a whale's flipper are short and strong for efficient steering.

Finger bones

A whale has finger bones, just like us.

Finger bones

Human bones

Compare a whale's flipper with a human's arm bones. Both have the same bones, but they are shaped differently.

The wolf of the sea

The orca, or killer whale, is sometimes known as the wolf of the sea because it is such a powerful hunter. It hunts all kinds of prey, including small fish, squid, penguins, and sea lions. It will even attack young blue whales.

A large male's dorsal fin can be as tall as an adult human being.

Orca facts

● Orcas are the largest members of the dolphin family.

● Female orcas live longer than males. They can live for 90 years. The males live for between 50 and 60 years.

● Orcas will knock ice floes to try and tip seals into the water.

The orca strikes so quickly that the sea lions are taken by surprise.

We are family!

Orcas live in close family groups called pods that stay together for life. A pod can vary from 6 to 40 whales, and has its own calls that each member recognizes.

Orcas, like other toothed whales, show many signs of intelligence.

An orca will herd a school of fish before picking them off, one by one.

A fast kill

Orcas are fast hunters, capable of reaching 30 mph (48 kph) when chasing prey. They will pick out fish, one by one, from a school, eating around 550 lb (250 kg) of food a day.

Shore attack

One population of orcas in Argentina has learned to beach themselves in order to grab an unwary sea lion; they then wriggle back into the sea. The skill is passed from one generation of orcas to the next.

Deep divers

Sperm whales are incredible divers. Having taken a breath, they head to the murky ocean floor in search of giant squid. A full-grown adult male will eat more than a ton of squid each day.

Going down
A sperm whale is able to dive as deep as 1.5 miles (2.5 km), although most dives are to about 1,200 ft (360 m).

A full-grown sperm whale is able to hold its breath for about 75 minutes.

What a big head!

The sperm whale's huge head is filled with oil. In the 1800s, sperm whales were hunted almost to extinction for this oil. The head can contain an amazing 500 gallons (1,900 liters)!

A giant squid may be 60 ft (19 m) long and have eyes the size of dinner plates.

Giant squid

Sperm whales often carry lots of egg-cup sized scars on their heads from the suckers of the giant squid.

Eye spy

The eye is tiny in proportion to the whale's body. Yet it is linked to the largest brain of any animal.

Moby Dick

The most famous sperm whale of all is Moby Dick, a rare white whale in a book by Herman Melville. This exciting story follows a sailor who hunts a whale after losing his leg to it.

The sea giant

Meet the largest animal alive today—
the blue whale. This animal is so large
that a bull elephant (the largest living
land animal) could sit on its tongue.
Other whales look tiny by comparison.

How big?
Everything about this whale is
big. Its flippers would stretch
from the floor to the ceiling
of your bedroom, while its
heart is the size of
a small car.

What a whopper!
At birth a blue whale is more than
a thousand times heavier than a
human baby. It will guzzle about
50 gallons (200 liters) of its
mother's milk every day. It puts
on the equivalent in weight of six
five-year-old children each day!

The blue whale can grow to

30

The blue whale is a baleen whale. It takes huge gulps of seawater and filters out the small fish and krill.

A snack for sharks

A blue whale may be big, but its size doesn't stop sharks and orcas from attacking it. This whale has lost a little bit of one of its tail flukes.

A big mouth

The blue whale's mouth is massive. Between 55 and 70 skin grooves or pleats run along the lower half from throat to mid-body. These expand when the whale gulps in its food.

90 ft (27 m) and weigh the same as 26 adult bull elephants.

Early whalers called the blue whale "sulfur bottom." Algae growing on its belly can make it appear yellow—the color of sulfur.

A fat chance of survival

The enormously fat walrus may look ungainly on land, but it is perfectly suited to life in the water. A thick layer of blubber protects it from the icy cold of its home in the Arctic Ocean.

I'll fight you!
Adult males will fight for space to be near females. However, despite looking nasty, these fights rarely result in serious injury.

A watery haven
The walrus loves the water. It uses its back flippers to push itself forward and its front flippers to change direction.

A walrus's tusk is an extra-long canine tooth.

Walrus tusks can grow to about 3 ft (1 m) in length.

Snuggle up
Walrus colonies are huge, with hundreds of members. It means there's a lot of jostling for position on the beach, but this also helps to keep the walruses warm.

A tooth story
Both males and females have tusks. Tusks are used for fighting, and the walrus also uses them to haul itself out of the water.

Fun in the water

These marine mammals are seals. Although they come onto land to rest and to give birth, they are most at home in the water, where they perform graceful underwater acrobatics.

True seals swim by moving their back flippers from side to side.

The short front flippers are used to steer the seal.

Eared seals have much longer front flippers than true seals.

True or not

Seals can be divided into two groups: true (or earless) seals and eared seals. True seals, such as these harbor seals, have no external ears.

Hear and move

Eared seals, such as this sea lion, have small external ears. They can also move around more easily on land and support themselves in a semi-upright position.

Breaking away

Harp seal pups triple their weight in the 12 days after their birth. Their mother then abandons them. After a month, they begin to lose their white coat for the adult gray fur.

Seals have often been mistaken for swimmers. Many legends tell of them coming ashore and behaving like people.

Like many mammals, seals like to play. It's a good way to learn.

Which is the biggest of all?

Male elephant seals are the largest of all seals, growing to 20 ft (6 m) and weighing more than 3.5 tons (3 metric tons).

The male elephant seals are some 10 times heavier than the females.

The sea cow

These creatures are dugongs and manatees, but they are also known as sea cows because of the way they graze on sea grass. In fact, they are the only vegetarian sea mammals.

Just looking for a quiet life

Manatees have paddle-shaped tails and live in warm shallow coastal waters, estuaries, and rivers.

Scarred for life

Because they are slow-moving, manatees are often killed or injured by boat propellers. Many carry the scars on their bodies or tails.

Mom! I'm here!

A manatee will give birth to a calf every two to three years. The bond between mother and baby is strong and is constantly reinforced with plenty of mouth contact.

The upper lip is very mobile.

Keep on eating

Sea cows are big eaters. They will gobble up to a quarter of their body weight in food every day.

Which is which?

Dugongs have crescent-shaped tails. It is the main visual difference between a dugong and a manatee.

A manatee's long flippers are used to hold food and push it toward the mouth.

Crescent-shaped tail

Weird and wonderful

Some whales look a little unusual.
The beluga is a white whale and has the
nickname of "sea canary." It can shape its
lips to make all kinds of sounds, including
barks, chirps, grunts, squeaks, and moos.

A color change
Belugas are born blue-gray
in color, but this turns to
white by the age of six.
They live in icy waters,
protected by a layer of
blubber as thick as
your hand is long.

Tusk defense

The narwhal's long tusk makes this whale easy to recognize. No one really knows what the tusk is for, especially since only the male narwhals have them. Biologists believe it may be used in fights to establish who is stronger.

A narwhal's tusk always spirals the same way. It can grow about 3 ft (1 m) in length and weigh over 20 lb (10 kg).

Under a microscope, whale lice look like tiny crabs.

A LITTLE BIT OF MAGIC

Around 600 years ago, sailors would return to port and sell narwhal tusks as unicorn horns. People believed that a unicorn horn had magical properties; cups made from them were supposed to stop a poison from working.

All aboard!

Some creatures make their home on a whale's skin. Baleen whales are often encrusted with barnacles and whale lice that nibble away at flakes of dead skin.

A large whale may be carrying as much as 1,000 lb (450 kg) of barnacles!

Marine mammals

Whales and dolphins are not the only marine mammals. Sea otters and polar bears are mammals that spend an awful lot of their time in the water—but, unlike whales and dolphins, they can also walk about on land.

Sailors have long called sea otters the "old men of the sea" because of their white whiskers and expressive faces.

What's for dinner?
Sea otters hunt in kelp forests for a range of seafood. They love to eat sea urchins, but will also munch on crabs, fish, squid, and mussels.

Sea otters are among the smallest marine mammals.

Fur, fur, and more fur
Sea otters have incredibly dense fur, which keeps them warm. In a patch of fur the size of your fingernail there are about 100,000 hairs—that's the same as the number of hairs on a human head!

Polar bears have been known to swim about 60 miles (100 km) in one stretch.

A polar bear lashes out as an Arctic fox, which is a land mammal, scoots by.

At home in the snow

A polar bear has hollow hairs, which keep the heat in. Combined with a thick layer of bear fat, they do not feel the cold of their Arctic home. If anything, they overheat!

Bear in the water

Polar bears are excellent swimmers, using their webbed paws to pull them along. In fact, their Latin name means "sea bear."

The otters anchor themselves to sea kelp.

Sea otters spend much of their time lying on their backs. They will even sleep and eat like this!

Whales in danger

In the past, fishermen used to hunt whales. So many died that there are hardly any left of some species. One of the problems is that their rate of reproduction is slow, so it is hard for them to recover from major losses.

Current danger

Whales are no longer hunted on a large scale, but they are threatened by our waste products. They become entangled in discarded fishing nets and suffer from oil spills. They are also exposed to pollution released into the sea from factories.

Are whales still caught?

Most countries have stopped whaling, but some continue to catch whales for scientific study. This ship has caught a minke whale and is pulling it up on deck.

AND ALL FOR A BRUSH...

In the 1800s and 1900s, one of the products that people wanted from whales was baleen. It was used for hair and floor brushes, combs, corsets, and umbrella frames. Its use gradually became unnecessary with the development of nylon, but it resulted in the deaths of thousands of whales.

What happened to the bowhead?

The bowhead was hunted almost to extinction in the 1800s, largely for its baleen, which can grow to more than 10 ft (3 m). It is thought that current population levels are around 10,000—from around 30,000 in the 1850s.

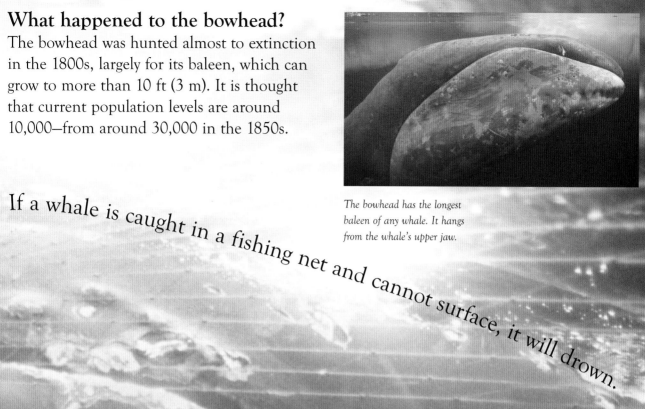

The bowhead has the longest baleen of any whale. It hangs from the whale's upper jaw.

If a whale is caught in a fishing net and cannot surface, it will drown.

Save the whale!

Whales have been around for more than 50 million years—that's about 10 times longer than human beings! Everyone wants them to stay around, and there are different ways of helping them to do so.

Some whales seem to be as curious about people as we are about them!

Let's go see a whale!
Some people like whales so much they want to see them up close. This is called whale watching. It has become a big business.

A path to freedom
These whales have become stranded underneath pack ice. The people are working to keep a breathing hole open and cut a path to the sea.

Without these people's help, the hole in the ice would soon freeze over, closing the whales' access to air.

The tag beams data to a satellite when the beluga surfaces. Tag attachment does not harm the whale.

Various organizations are working hard to save whale populations by making people more aware of issues such as whaling, overfishing, and water pollution.

How can we help them?

There is a lot that we don't know about whales, including where they go and how many there are. Satellite tags are useful for helping to track a whale's movements. They fall off after a few weeks.

Where are you?

Help! An orca calf has lost his mom. Answer the questions correctly to guide him safely through the ice.

Beluga

Gray whale

Sperm whale

Blue whale

Which whale makes a 12,000-mile (20,000-km) journey?
See page 22

schools

Like all whales, **orcas** live in family groups called...
See page 27

pods

packs

START

Whales are...
See page 4

fish

FINISH

This whale is
known as the **wolf**
of the sea.
See page 26

Orca

Gray whales

Humpback whale

Beluga

Orca

Narwhal

Which whale has
two blow holes?
See page 6

Humpback whale

Blue whale

mammals

Which whale has
a long tusk?
See page 39

amphibians

47

Facts matchup

How much do you know about the mammals of the sea? Each of these mammals can be found in the book—read the clues and see if you can identify the correct mammal.

Harbor seal

Walrus

Beluga

Dugong

Polar bear

Sea otters

Bottlenose dolphin

There are about 26 different types, or species, of my kind. **See page 12**

This grows up to 8 in (20 cm) in length. **See page 15**

I can move on land but not very easily. I don't have tusks. **See page 34**

I have extremely dense fur that keeps me warm. **See page 40**

This is smooth and rubbery to touch. It is made up of two sections, or flukes. **See page 10**

A hardy swimmer, my kind have been known to swim about 60 miles (100 km) in one stretch. **See page 41**

I live in a huge colony and space is tight. I make good use of my long tusks when necessary. **See page 33**

I **have** small ears and long flippers and can move around fairly easily on land. **See page 34**

I **have** a paddle-shaped tail and am related to the dugong. **See page 36**

We **filter feeders** fish in groups of up to 25. **See page 16**

Shaped like a torpedo, I am the fastest sea mammal of all. **See page 9**

Sperm whale's tooth

Manatee

Humpback whale

Orca

Blue whale

Whale's tail

Narwhal

Sea lion

Sperm whale

I **spend** most of the year in icy polar waters. My favorite food is squid. **See page 22**

I **have** a crescent-shaped tail and am related to the manatee. **See page 37**

I **have** a long, heavy tusk. It distinguishes me from other whales. **See page 39**

I **can moo** but I am not a cow. I can squeak but I am not a mouse. Who am I? **See page 38**

I **am** the world's largest animal. My heart is as big as a small car. **See page 30**

Who am I?

Take a look at these close-ups of mammals in the book and see if you can identify them. The clues should help you!

➤ Though tiny in size...

➤ ...I am food to some whales.

➤ I am no longer than your finger.

See page 16

➤ I find food with the help of my sensitive whiskers.

➤ White fur helps me to hide from danger.

See page 5

➤ I have incredibly dense fur.

➤ I am one of the smallest marine mammals.

See page 40

➤ I am a toothed whale.

➤ I have only one blowhole.

See page 6

➤ I live in the Arctic Ocean.

➤ My tusks can grow up to 3 ft (1 m) in length.

See page 33

50

➤ If I lose a tooth, it cannot be replaced.

➤ I can have up to 100 teeth.

See page 14

➤ My favorite food is sea grass.

➤ I live in warm, shallow waters.

See page 36

➤ I have the largest brain of any animal.

➤ I can hold my breath for more than an hour.

See pages 28–29

➤ I am born blue-gray in color and turn white later.

➤ I have a nickname: "sea canary."

See page 38

➤ I have a long beak.

➤ I can turn my head.

➤ I have tiny eyes.

See page 13

➤ I can swim 10 times faster than you can walk.

➤ An elephant could sit on my tongue.

See page 31

Treasure hunt

Get ready for a deep dive in this exciting game. Avoid dangers on the way as you race your friends to be the first to reach the treasure chest.

Oxygen low.
Move back 5

Hitch a ride on a passing submarine.
Move forward 4

Get caught in a fishing net.
Skip a turn

Humpback whales migration. Change direction.
Move back 2

Swim faster to keep up with a sea cow.
Move forward 6

How to play

This game is for up to four players.

You will need
A die
Counters—one for each player

Move up **Move down**

Trace over the diver outlines above, or make your own from cardboard. Players begin from the START box and take turns throwing the die. Follow the squares with each roll. If you land on an instruction, do as it says. Good luck!

A hungry seal blocks your way. **Skip a turn**

Sea currents are in your favor. **Move forward 2**

START

A pod of whales is coming your way. **Move back 4**

Find a route map. **Move forward 6**

You spy the treasure and speed up. **Move forward 5**

FINISH

A sperm whale is hunting squid. **Move back 5**

Glossary

Here are the meanings of some words that are useful to know
when learning about whales and dolphins.

Baleen a black, brushlike material that hangs down from the upper jaw of a baleen (or toothless) whale. It is used for straining krill and plankton from the sea.

Beak the pronounced snout that most whales and dolphins have.

Blow the small cloud of spray produced when a whale surfaces and opens its blowhole.

Blowhole the entrance to a whale's nasal passages, found on top of its head.

Blubber the layer of oily fat under the skin that keeps a whale warm.

Breach a leap performed by a whale when it jumps up from the water and splashes back down.

Bubble nets are sometimes created by humpback whales to help them to catch fish.

Dorsal fin the fin on the back of most whales and dolphins.

Echolocation a method used by dolphins and some whales to find food or obstacles. They send out a sound and wait for the returning echo.

Extinction the death of a species.

Marine mammals depend on the sea for survival. They can all dive, but must come to the surface for air.

Migration the journey a whale makes to find a better feeding or breeding ground, often depending on seasonal changes.

Pod a family of whales.

Species a group of animal that shares certain unique characteristics.

Suckle the means by which a baby mammal takes milk from its mother by sucking a nipple.

Whaling the hunting and killing of whales.

Index

Picture credits

The publisher would like to thank the following for their kind permission to reproduce their photographs:

a=above; c=center; b=below; l=left; r=right; t=top; Bkg=background

Alamy Images: Bryan and Cherry Alexander Photography 41tr; Greg Balfour Evans 46bl, 47tr; Image State/Martin Ruegner 12c; Heather Angel/Natural Visions: Tony Martin 45br; Ardea London Ltd: Jean-Paul Ferrero 23br; Francois Gohier 3r, 4b, 6br, 44c, 46t; Ken Lucas 39cl; D. Parer and E. Parer-Cook 26b; Ron and Valerie Taylor 22bl; Bruce Coleman Inc: Mark Newman 41tl; Phillip Colla/OceanLight.com: 10tl, 11tc, 11tr, 11cl, 17tl, 17tr, 22tl, 31tr, 34bl; Corbis: Ralph A. Clevenger 34Bkg; Brandon D. Cole 20c; Peter Johnson 5tr, 16tl, 50tr; Denis Scott 49c; Robert Marien 14bl, 51bl; Joe McDonald 35tr; Amos Nachoum 27cr; Richard T. Nowitz 24c; Jeffrey L. Rotman 9c, 19br, 29br; Ron Sanford 16b; Kevin Schafer 5br, 33tr, 33br, 50c, 50clb, 51br; Stuart Westmorland 10b; Dorling Kindersley: Hunstanton Sea Life Centre, Hunstanton, Norfolk 59cla; Imperial War Museum, London 52cl, 59bc; Natural History Museum, London 46cr, 48cr, 49cb, 58cl, 59clb; University

Museum of Zoology, Cambridge 49cl, 58cb, 59cr, 59bl (Orca, skeleton); Dreamstime.com: Filip Fuxa 49clb; Wayne Johnson 49tc; Vladimir Seliverstov 48cl; Getty Images: 1c, 4c, 7br, 10tl, 18b, 19tr, 20b, 27tr, 38c, 40b; Photodisc/Keren 59cra; Purestock 59cla (Harp Seal); Kevin Schafer/The Image Bank 50bl; Art Wolfe/Iconica 50cl, 51cl; National Geographic/Robert Rosing 33l; naturepl.com: Edwin Giesbers 14-15bc; Todd Pusser 51c; SeaPics.com: Doug Perrine 51tc, 51bc; Doc White 51tr; Greenpeace Inc: 43br; Hunstanton Sea Life Centre: 34c; Natural History Museum: 39tr; Nature Picture Library: Doug Allan 2t, 15tr; Peter Bassett 35br; Brandon Cole 18c; Jeff Foott 32c; Martha Holmes 43tr; Todd Pusser 13cr, 39b; Tom Walmsley 8tl; Doc White 6t; Seapics.com: Bryan and Cherry Alexander 42c; Robin W. Baird 15l; Drew Bradley 21tl; Phillip Colla 30bl; Bob Cranston 8b; Goran Ehlme 23tr; John K.B. Ford/Ursus 39c; Armin Maywald 13tl; Hiroya Minakuchi 26c; Michael S. Nolan 13b; Doug Perrine 13tr, 28l, 29bl, 29t, 34tl, 34b, 35c, 35br; Robert L. Pitman 5cl; Masa Ushioda 11cb, 20tl, 21bl, 48; Doc White 31c, 40tl; S.M.R.U: 15br; Still Pictures: Mark Cawardine 10tr; Michael Sewell 41br; University Museum of Zoology, Cambridge: 14t.

Humpback whale images taken under, and published according to, the provisions of NMFS scientific research permit 882. Phillip Colla/Hawaii Whale Research Foundation.

All other images © Dorling Kindersley
For further information see: www.dkimages.com